MW01244753

Made in the USA
Middletown, DE
29 March 2022

63362285R00064